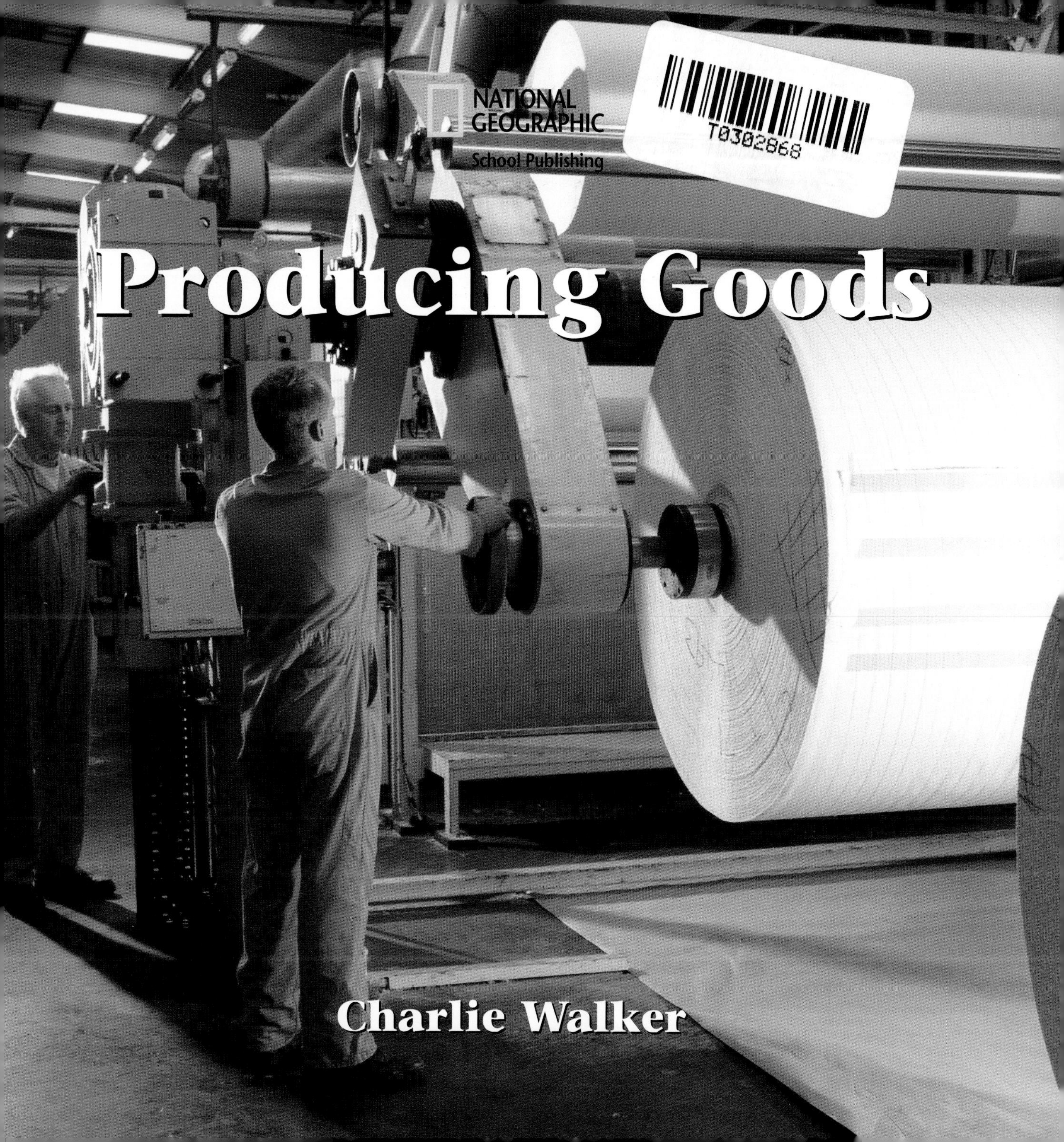

NATIONAL GEOGRAPHIC
School Publishing

Producing Goods

Charlie Walker

PICTURE CREDITS
Cover, 1, 4 (left below and right), 5 (right below), 7 (above and left below), 8, 9 (below), 10, 11 (right and below), 13 (above and right), 14, 17 (above right), 19 (above and below), 20 (left below), 20 (right center and right below), Photolibrary.com; 3 (left), 7 (right below), 12, 17 (below), 21 (right below), Getty Images; 4 (left above), 9 (right), 11 (above), 13 (below), 16 (right), 18, 20 (center below), APL/Corbis; 5 (right above), Alaska Stock LLC/Alamy; 6 and 16 (left) , Helene Rogers/Alamy; 15 (above), Jeff Greenberg/Alamy; 15 (below), John Powell Photographer/Alamy; 9 (above), CSIRO; 17 (left above and right) Dorling Kindersley.

Produced through the worldwide resources of the National Geographic Society, John M. Fahey, Jr., President and Chief Executive Officer; Gilbert M. Grosvenor, Chairman of the Board; Nina D. Hoffman, Executive Vice President and President, Books and Education Publishing Group.

PREPARED BY NATIONAL GEOGRAPHIC SCHOOL PUBLISHING
Steve Mico, Executive Vice President and Publisher, Children's Books and Education Publishing Group; Marianne Hiland, Editor in Chief; Lynnette Brent, Executive Editor; Michael Murphy and Barbara Wood, Senior Editors; Nicole Rouse, Editor; Bea Jackson, Design Director; David Dumo, Art Director; Shanin Glenn, Designer; Margaret Sidlosky, Illustrations Director; Matt Wascavage, Manager of Publishing Services; Sean Philpotts, Production Manager.

MANUFACTURING AND QUALITY MANAGEMENT
Christopher A. Liedel, Chief Financial Officer; Phillip L. Schlosser, Vice President; Clifton M. Brown III, Director.

BOOK DEVELOPMENT
Ibis for Kids Australia Pty Limited.

Published by the National Geographic Society
1145 17th Street, N.W.
Washington, D.C. 20036-4688

Product No. 4W1005062

ISBN-13: 978-1-4263-5058-0
ISBN-10: 1-4263-5058-9

2018
4 5 6 7 8 9 10 11 12 13 14 15

Printed in the USA

Contents

Think and Discuss

Talk about these products, or goods. What things from nature were used to make them?

Where Do Goods Come From?

Many **goods** that people need and want are made from **raw materials** found in nature.

Pottery is made from clay. Clay comes from the ground.

Wool clothing is made from sheep's wool.

Cotton clothing is made from cotton plants.

Ice cream is made from cow's milk.

Most paper is made from the wood of trees.

From Sheep to Woolly Socks

A sheep's wool is a raw material. Wool is used to make many goods, including clothes. Wool goes through many steps to become woolen goods.

Sheep grow a wool coat. Once a year the wool is cut off the sheep. This is called shearing.

The wool is taken to a **factory**. At the factory the wool is combed using huge **machines** to make it smooth.

The wool is made into yarn and dyed different colors.

The yarn is knitted together to make woolen goods, such as these woolly socks.

From Cotton Plant to Cotton Shirt

A cotton plant is a raw material. Cotton is used to make many goods, including clothes. Cotton goes through many steps to become cotton goods.

Cotton plants grow seedpods that are full of cotton. Farmers **harvest** the cotton using a cotton picker.

The cotton is sent to a factory. At the factory it is cleaned and combed. This makes the cotton smooth.

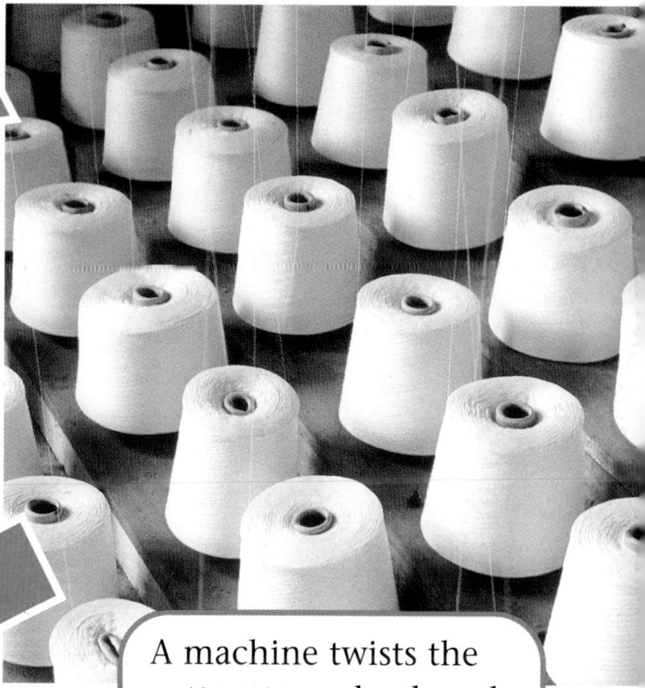

A machine twists the cotton to make thread.

The thread is woven together to make fabric. The fabric is made into goods, such as this cotton T-shirt.

From Wood to Paper

Wood from trees is a raw material. Wood is used to make many goods, including paper. Wood goes through many steps to become paper.

Some trees are grown in forests just to make paper. The trees are cut down, ground up, and sent to a paper mill.

The wood shavings are mixed with water to make pulp. The pulp is put on large, hot rollers to dry.

The large rolls of paper are cut into sheets of paper.

The paper is made into goods, such as this book.

From Dairy Cows to Ice Cream

Milk from a cow is a raw material. People drink milk and use it to make many goods, including ice cream. Milk goes through many steps to become ice cream.

Cows **produce** milk. The cows are milked, usually by machine.

The milk is sent to factories. It is mixed with other ingredients and frozen to make ice cream.

The ice cream is packaged in tubs.

People buy and eat the ice cream.

From Clay to Pots

Clay from the earth is a raw material. Clay is used to make many goods, including pottery. Clay goes through many steps to become pottery.

Clay is dug up from below the ground. When it is wet, it becomes soft and can be shaped.

There are different ways of working with clay. Often, it is shaped on a potter's wheel.

The clay objects are put into a hot oven called a kiln. The heat hardens the clay.

Many beautiful and useful **products** are made from clay.

From Trees to Tires

Latex from rubber trees is a raw material. The latex is used to make rubber, which can be used to make many goods, including tires. The rubber goes through many steps to become tires.

Rubber trees produce a sticky fluid called latex. The latex is collected from the trees.

The latex is put through large rollers that squeeze the water out and flatten the latex into sheets. These sheets are dried and packaged.

The latex is sent to factories. The latex is mixed with chemicals and made into tires.

Rubber tires are used for many different kinds of vehicles, including cars.

Use What You Learned

woolen clothes

tires

pots

newspapers

What raw materials were used to produce the goods shown below?

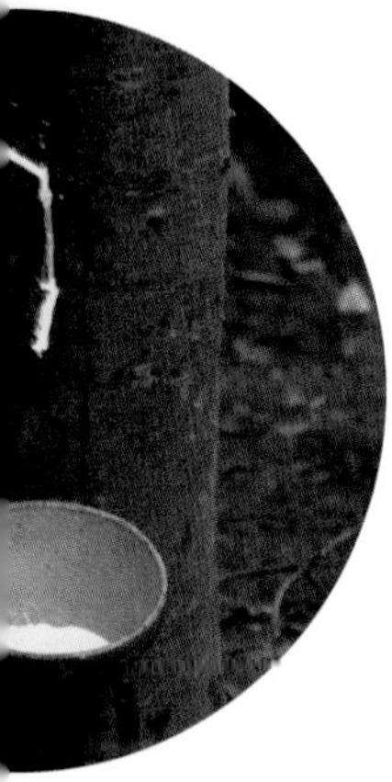

factory

goods

harvest

machine

product

raw material

Glossary

KEY CONCEPT

factory (page 9)
A place where raw materials are processed
Wool is combed and made into yarn in a factory.

KEY CONCEPT

goods (page 6)
Any product that can be sold
Many goods that people need and want are made from raw materials found in nature.

KEY CONCEPT

harvest (page 10)
To gather crops of something
Farmers harvest cotton with a cotton picker.

KEY CONCEPT

machine (page 9)
Something with several parts that work together to do a job
A machine twists cotton to make thread.

produce (page 14)
Turn raw materials into finished goods
Milk is used to produce ice cream.

KEY CONCEPT

product (page 17)
Something that is made or grown for people to use
Pottery products are made from clay.

KEY CONCEPT

raw material (page 6)
Any material found in nature that is used to make products
Workers must follow a sequence of steps to turn a raw material into a finished product that can be sold.

Index